Living Broad

Shirley Rutter

BookLeaf Publishing

India | USA | UK

Presentation by *BookLeaf Publishing*

Web: www.bookleafpub.com

E-mail: info@bookleafpub.com

ISBN: 9789358317602

First edition 2023

As heavenward I oft times look

For you, my mother is this book.

For love and oft remembered times

For you, my father, are my rhymes.

And for my children, poems could be

Just one more way to remember me.

Inspired by life and love and friends,

My thoughts, my words, with love are sent.

ACKNOWLEDGEMENT

I wouldn't be here without the excellent
treatment from out wonderful NHS, underpinned
with an extraordinary amount of love and
support from family, friends, and local residents.

PREFACE

From being diagnosed with Breast Cancer in 1997, no-one is more surprised than I to be writing this in 2023.

Voices

One small voice wants to feel sad
Feel bad, wallow in a circumstance Beyond
control.
Cry a little, try so little...
Only a small voice wanting to pay
The price for being a human Doing
Not a human Being.
Believing in only one speed.
Not trusting
To be effective at a lesser speed.
But a bigger voice, amplified by
The spirit of love and friendship,
The quality and quantity of which
Take my breath away...
And make me want to shout so loudly
With my last breath
Thank-you! Thank-you! Thank-you!
Let me live to live to a higher purpose.
Let me touch your lives with more love
Than you imagine.
As you have touched mine.
The bigger voice WILL be heard,
With your help, from the mountain tops...
The small voice recedes, defeated.

Extra Time

Twelve months have passed and I'm still here
Those early days, so full of fear
Those early nights spent fighting tears,
And being brave as dawn drew near.

Grateful for each passing day,
Thankful for the chance to say...
Amazed by love that's come my way,
Determined that love to repay.

So many things I need to do,
To live each day and work things through
To live and learn from lessons new,
To respect my different point of view.

I bless the lump that has made me
Stop, and look,and clearly see
What life's about, at least for me
To be the best that I can be.

To think, to read, to love and play,
To laugh, to give, to work and pray
To make the most of every day
And bless the good' that's come my way.

Post Operative Lament

Oooh… I wish I could sleep on my side
Curl up, and be foetal and hide
From the swelling, the pain, shy away from life's
rain,
I wish I could sleep on my side!

Oooh to roll over and snuggle
Tucked up with a soft toy to cuddle
Not be flat on my back, as if on the rack
Oooh to roll over and snuggle.

On my back little sleep can be sought
I'm brought rudely awake with a snort !
My nasal contortions reach Olympic proportions
On my back little sleep can be sought.

Time passes, time heals, yes it's true
Two weeks or so, long overdue...
Hadn't thought, hadn't tried, but woke up on my
side!
Time passes, time heals, yes it's true.

Don't sweat the Big Stuff

To whom...etc...etc
Thank you for your kind offer
All points of which
I have given due consideration.

It was "Tails"
Sorry.

Resolution Day

So far, today, I've done just fine,
I've thanked the Lord for me and mine,
I haven't moaned or lost my patience,
Made bad choice, shown lack of good sense...
Haven't gossiped, haven't lied
Stamped my foot or taken sides...
Not been grumpy, not been curt
Not been thoughtless, no-one's hurt.
Not had junk food, fags or wine
Not been lazy, wasting time...
Haven't sworn and haven't binged
Haven't made a mess of things...

So please Lord, help it stay that way
As I leave my bed to start the day!

.

Growing Pains

It takes courage to think for yourself,
It takes more to do it aloud..
To stand alone, convinced, inspired
Oblivious to the crowd.

My Friend

Thank you for being my friend.
Thank you for the times when
No words
Have been enough,
And for the times when we've had
Infinite things to say
All in the safety and comfort
That the important words will be
Salvaged and preserved,
And the rubbish will be
Swept away and promptly forgotten.
I dare to be myself,
You dare to be yourself.
You respect my bad decisions
And you don't make me justify them,
Or remind me I was foolish.

And through my darker days,
When you thought you were powerless to help,
Your existence,
Your heartfelt kindness
Carried me through the confusion
And lifted me into the light.

And in return
If I could work magic,
It would be for you.

Give Gratefully

Give gratefully to.'Breakthrough'
Then great progress can be made...
Huge leaps and bounds in research
Means more lives will be saved.

Your valued contribution,
However small it seems,
If multiplied by many
May fulfil one of my dreams.

I believe with all our efforts,
The battle can be won
To reduce the monthly death rate
From one thousand, down to NONE.

Then those who are our mothers,
Partners, sisters, daughters too
May stay near us for much longer
And live full lives anew.

Give gratefully to 'Breakthrough'
Great progress IS being made...
Let's make this disease 'history''
Our contribution well repaid.

*'Breakthrough Breast Cancer' metamorphed into
'Breast Cancer Now'

Trekking Annapurna

I look ahead.
The steep winding track reaches the horizon.
The physical and rhythmic energy
As one step follows another
Enables the healing to begin.
Thoughts expand and
Focus shifts to the surrounding
And snow capped mountains
Peep and peak.
It's so beautiful before me,
It's so peaceful above me...
I stop, and notice, and feel...
A greater power is all around.
It is always there, but sometimes I
Distance myself from IT.
The healing connection soothes me
As I trek the winding track
Which leads me back to me.

* Fundraising Trek, November 2000

Paperback Writer

Oh to be the well travelled
Traveller's book.
The dog-eared splayed pages
A testimony to fulfilled purpose!
Title faded down crinkled spine...
Revealed, understood, if time and close
inspection
Are allowed.
Experienced to command
Twice the space between eager
Less read colleagues
Never more to be fully closed.
Versatile enough to be a mug or wine glass
coaster,
If required.
Flexible enough to be folded inside out
To be read one-handed in bed,
If required.

Well loved, well used, enjoyed, taken, sniffed,
traded..
Real and individual grit between the pages...

Not for ME to be carefully kept,
Occasionally, unnecessarily dusted
On a pristine shelf.

My Special Friends

Some friends are old, some friendships new,
But all have shaped my point of view,
They give a shining light that guides
When my light, in the darkness hides.

I'm proud to say, I'm proud it's true
The love of friends has seen me through,
They send a shining light that guides
When my hope in the darkness hides.

An honesty is now in view
A simple faith I never knew,
I sense the shining light that guides
When my dreams in the darkness hide.

Much love and thanks I feel are due
I'm who I am because of you,
I have a shining light that guides
When my life in the darkness hides.

Stumbling Thro'

*Denzil is a very big, very black cat!

"What's that, Granma?" asked Charlotte, (three),
Tracing a scar where some breast used to be...
"Did Denzil scratch you?" "No" smiled I,
"Did you fall off your bike ? Did you crash? Did
you cry ?"

"No, nothing like that, sweetheart"
I replied
As she tugged at my top and peered inside...
"Does it hurt?" She asked with sympathetic
breath
"Not now", said I (though I've felt hurt to death)

"The nice man at the hospital made me well
I'm all better now, as you can tell..."

I don't care a jot that it doesn't 'look nice'
Surviving breast cancer not once, but thrice
Makes me value life, and love, and health
Oh the joy of 'being here' to tell her myself.

2007

Parenting

My gifts to you before I die
Are roots to ground you
And wings to fly...
There's such a lot of world to see
Go on, enjoy, be spirits free.
I try to teach you what I know
Learning from you, as we go...
Think for yourselves, find yourselves
Develop intuition true,
Be independent, you are unique
Rely and trust your point of view.

Achieve all this, and my job's done,
I'll rest in peace, the proudest Mum.

December 2000

Autumn

The last leaves drip from naked tree,
And conkered children shriek and yell,
And little wellingtons trudge and kick
Delighting in the colours, and the smell
Of Autumn.

Out mitts and scarves come out to play,
'Til pale sun sinks in red sky mass,
And porridge speeds to chocolate drink
As days grow short and quickly pass
In Autumn.

Come home to fire's welcome glow
And casserole cooking on the stove,
Hot water bottles with tops turned tight,
A season that I'll always love
Is Autumn.

Perfect Date

Punctually called for.
Then we strolled hand in hand
To the local Theatre.
A spontaneous stop with an Artist
For a caricature en route.
The show was great, and after
We giggled and chatted as we
Walked to The Wine Bar for supper.
Then home.
Candle lit bedroom and cosy games
'Till one of us fell asleep.
(I think it was me).

I stretched awake refreshed and happy
And we hugged and smiled smugly.
I showered as breakfast was prepared
And we reunited in the big brass bed.

Dressing leisurely and planning next weekend,
We parted.

I am Charlotte, nearly six.

If my Granma can't find a man like her...
She'll settle for a Granma like mine !!

*baby Charlotte will be 21 next March...How lucky
am I to still 'be here' and the bond is just as strong?!

The Storm

Dark clouds looming
Thunder booming
Raindrops falling
Mothers calling
Children dashing
Lightening flashing
Will it never end ??

Fowl seek shelter
Heater skelter
Flowers are drooping
Dripping stooping
Rain falls faster
Drums disaster
Will it never end ??

*Printed in the school magazine, aged 13

Loneliness

The bed is cold.
The dark is hateful.
A shroud of emptiness envelops
The shivering, hopeless body.
Alone and lonely, smothered
By a heartless night blanket.
The warmth of the morning, a blissful
Too distant horizon.
Time away.
Too tired to sleep.
Too alone to cry...
Just waiting for the sun
And for you.

Winter Seaside

The wind whipped up the
Top veneer of sand
And made it run and linger like disco smoke
Over the puddled expanse of beach.
Then resting, as suddenly as it was roused.
And above, the wind whipped
The bottom veneer of cloud
And made it chase across the sky.
No resting there, they still chase and chase.
The tide is coming in, in grey, relentless waves,
Encroaching ever nearer,
Lapping louder, spray and rain blending noisily
into one.
Seagulls bustle and squawk
Like ladies assembling for a jumble sale.
Collar up, and hands thrust deeper into pockets
While trousers flutter damply around bracing
legs.
Cheeks flushed, glowing, yet cold to touch.

Enjoying the moment all the more, in the
knowledge
That a hot drink waits.

Bertie Bartram

Bertie Bartram spent his time
Cultivating spoken rhyme,
Whene'er he talked to one and all
Poetry from his lips would fall.
His couplets drove his poor wife spare
And greyness flourished in her hair
She'd close her eyes and count to three
Then ask, what would he like for tea?
"Perhaps I'd like some cheese on toast,
Or beans, whichever you'd like most
And then some fruit with cream or jelly,
To fill a corner of my belly
And if, my love, you've time to bake
A scone or two and a slice of cake"

To the kitchen she would fly
As anger blazed from flashing eye
Her stifled scream was barely heard
And really, it was quite absurd!
The simplest routine daily chores
Were marred by awful rhymes - of course
Bertie thought himself quite grand
And half expected all the land
To flock and gather at his gate
For just a glimpse of the Poet Laureate!

He'd sign an autograph, or two
And say some clever lines, a few
Well chosen words to make them smile
Before he'd have to rest awhile.

Then, one day, pride behoved a fall
When Bertie heard his good wife call
And in the hallway, there he found
His wife, with cases, all around. "Well, my dear,
what's going on?
Are you leaving? What on earth is wrong ?
You cannot leave a man like me
Besides, now who will do my tea ?"
"You'll help yourself!" Came the reply
"I want to LIVE before I die
I can stand no more of your naff verse
Life with you has been a curse.
I'm off to live with Mr. Rose
To spend my last days talking prose !"

Weigh to go !

I've shaved my legs,
And armpits too,
Forced a wee
And strained a pooh...
Plucked my eyebrows
Blown my nose,
Removed nail varnish from my toes.
Plucked some nose hair
Filed my nails...

I'm ready ! Lead me
To those scales.

*sponsored slim event

Poetry Appreciation

*No-one can make your words inferior without your consent!

Oooh! I couldn't write anything like that !
Oooh! I wouldn't write anything like that!
Oooh! Maybe I could write something like that...
Oooh! Maybe I could write something.
Oooh! Maybe I could write.
Oooh ! Maybe I could.
Oooh! Maybe I…
Maybe…
Oooh!...
    I did !

www.ingramcontent.com/pod-product-compliance
Lightning Source LLC
Chambersburg PA
CBHW071244140726
47996CB00007B/2744